Contents

*Words in **bold** are explained in the glossary on page 30.*

My friend Katy

Katy (in the red T-shirt) has had asthma since she was four years old.

I'm Zara and this is my friend Katy. She lives with her mum and little sister, Laura, two streets away from me.

After school, I usually go to Katy's house for an hour or two. Katy's mum makes us a snack when we get in.

"Hallo Zara," she says. "How are you? Would you like some toast?" When we've finished eating, we go upstairs to listen to music or read a magazine. I like Katy's bedroom, even though it's different from mine. There are no curtains and no carpet – not even a rug. Instead she has window blinds and a wooden floor. I like her floor because it's slippery and fun to slide on in socks.

MY FRIEND has Asthma

BY ANNA LEVENE

Chrysalis Children's Books

First published in the UK in 2003 by
Chrysalis Children's Books
64 Brewery Road,
London N7 9NT

ISBN 1 84138 838 6

British Library Cataloguing in Publication Data for this book is available
from the British Library.

A BELITHA BOOK

Editorial Manager: Joyce Bentley
Senior Editor: Sarah Nunn
Project Editor: Sue Nicholson
Designer: Wladek Szechter
Photographer: Michael Wicks
Picture researcher: Terry Forshaw
Illustrations: Tom Connell

Consultant: National Asthma Campaign
*The National Asthma Campaign is a UK charity working to conquer asthma. To find out more about the charity,
contact the office listed on page 31.*

The photographer and publishers would like to thank Anoli; Daisy; Pam Davies; Ochre; Christine,
James and Victoria Pearson; Joshua Rosenheim; Sophie Ryan; Tom and Val Wicks; and Buckingham College,
Pinner, for their help in preparing this book.

Picture acknowledgements:
5 (bottom), Eye of Science/Science Photo Library; 21 (bottom), Digital Vision; 29, Peter Cade/Getty Images

Printed in Hong Kong

10 9 8 7 6 5 4 3 2 1

Katy's mum vacuums Katy's room every other day to get rid of dust.

She also wipes down the blinds and the furniture, and mops the floor. I once asked her if she liked cleaning. She laughed and said she did it to help stop Katy coughing.

"It's because Katy has asthma," she said, "and dust is one of the things that makes Katy cough."

Katy and Zara are best friends. After tea, they often read in Katy's room. It has a wooden floor to cut down on dust. Dust makes Katy cough.

ASTHMA FACTS

DUST MITES

The word asthma comes from Ancient Greek. It means "to breathe hard". Many people with asthma find it difficult to breathe easily if exposed to dust – or, more precisely, to the droppings of tiny insects called **house dust mites**, which live in dust. Even in the cleanest houses, dust is trapped in carpets, curtains, bedding and chair covers. So it's often easier to replace them with furnishings that can be wiped down with a cloth.

Magnified picture of a house dust mite, shown several hundred times larger than its real size.

Symptoms and triggers

Coughing for a long time is very tiring, and can make you feel ill.

Katy's cough is a **symptom** of her asthma. She gets other symptoms, too. For example, when she breathes, she sometimes makes a kind of whistling noise in her chest. This is called wheezing. It can sound quite funny. But if Katy's symptoms get worse, her chest starts to feel tight and she can't breathe properly. That's not funny at all – although Katy always has special medicine with her to help her breathe normally again.

Katy's symptoms are caused by an **allergy.** I know because my mum told me. She said that if you have an allergy, your body reacts to something around you that doesn't bother anyone else.

Anything that sets off asthma symptoms is called a **trigger**. Not everyone has the same triggers. Like many people with asthma, Katy is allergic to dust. Her asthma symptoms are also triggered if she catches a cold.

Many people with asthma are allergic to household pets.

ASTHMA FACTS

COMMON ASTHMA TRIGGERS

- a cold or the flu
- house dust mite droppings and furry or feathery animals, such as dogs, cats and hamsters
- pollen from grasses
- energetic exercise, particularly outdoors when the weather is cold and dry
- cigarette smoke
- sudden changes in the weather

ALLERGIES

People can be allergic to all sorts of things. Some people react to certain foods, such as nuts, wheat or shellfish. Other people have allergies to medicine, such as penicillin. Whatever someone is allergic to is called an **allergen**.

Some people are allergic to nuts.

How you breathe

You need to breathe to live. Most of the time you breathe without thinking about it. Air enters your body through your nose or mouth and travels down your **windpipe** into your lungs. There, it goes through a series of tubes called **airways**, or bronchi, into tiny air sacs called alveoli. Oxygen in the air passes out of these air sacs and into your bloodstream. Your blood then carries the oxygen around your body to where it is needed. Your body needs oxygen to live and grow.

People with asthma have airways that are almost always swollen and inflamed, although they are not painful. But if something irritates the airways, the muscles around the airway walls tighten so that the airways become narrower. At the same time, the lining to the airways swells and produces a sticky fluid called **mucus**. The mucus clogs the airways and makes them even narrower than before. This makes it hard to breathe.

This man has come into contact with something that has triggered his asthma. The airways in his lungs have become narrower, making it difficult for him to breathe.

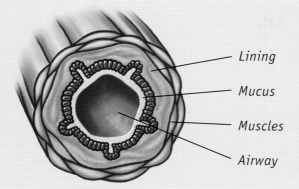

- Lining
- Mucus
- Muscles
- Airway

A wide, healthy airway of someone without asthma.

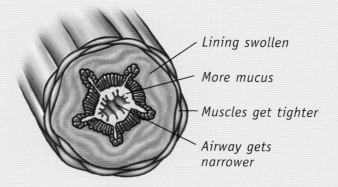

- Lining swollen
- More mucus
- Muscles get tighter
- Airway gets narrower

A narrow airway of someone with asthma.

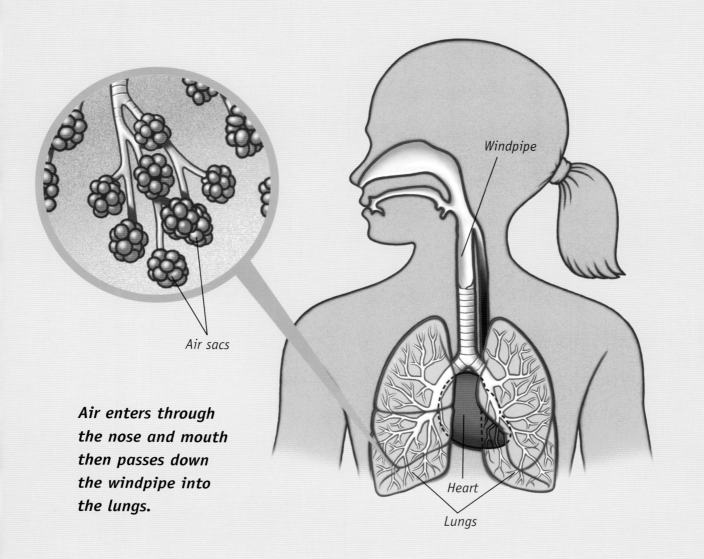

Air sacs

Air enters through the nose and mouth then passes down the windpipe into the lungs.

Windpipe

Heart

Lungs

Relievers

Katy and I love sport. We've both been picked for our school netball team. Now we spend hours every weekend practising in Katy's garden.

About ten minutes before we start, Katy takes some medicine to stop her becoming wheezy. It comes in a small blue tube a bit like a mini spray can. It's called an **inhaler**, or puffer. Katy fits her inhaler into the end of a large plastic container called a **spacer**. She puts the other end of the spacer into her mouth. When she clicks the inhaler, a **dose** of medicine goes into the spacer and Katy breathes it in.

It makes a sort of fizzy, whooshing sound. I once asked Katy if I could have a go, but she thought I'd better not.

The medicine in the blue inhaler is called a **reliever**. Katy uses it if she starts to feel any asthma symptoms, or if she's going to do any sport. Katy makes sure she's always got her inhaler with her and that there's always plenty of medicine inside.

Opposite: **Katy uses her reliever inhaler before she starts playing netball to make sure the exercise does not trigger her asthma symptoms.**

Katy breathes in her medicine through a special plastic container called a spacer. The spacer is easier to use than an inhaler alone. It's also better at getting the medicine into her lungs.

ASTHMA FACTS

WHAT ARE RELIEVERS FOR

Relievers are used to ease, or relieve, the symptoms of asthma so that they do not develop into a serious asthma attack. Relievers relax the muscles around the airways in the lungs. The airways then open up, making it easier to breathe.

Preventers

Katy told me that every morning and evening she has to take another kind of medicine, even if she feels well. This medicine is called a **preventer**. She started taking it a few months ago when her asthma got worse. Her doctor thinks it worsened because she had a lot of colds last winter.

Katy's preventer inhaler is a different colour from her reliever inhaler so

*Opposite: **After Katy has taken her preventer medicine, she brushes her teeth to make sure none of the medicine is left in her mouth.***

that she doesn't get the two muddled up. She uses her spacer to take her preventer asthma medicine, just like she does for her reliever medicine.

Katy likes using the spacer because she doesn't have to worry about pressing the inhaler and breathing in at exactly the same time.

ASTHMA FACTS

KINDS OF INHALER

There are many different designs of inhaler, both for preventer and reliever medicine. One looks a bit like a mini disk recorder. Another looks like a compact disc player.

WHAT ARE PREVENTERS FOR?

Preventers are taken to control swelling in the airways so they are not so sensitive. They therefore help to prevent a serious asthma attack. However, preventers need time to work. That is why they need to be taken every day.

This boy is using a square-shaped inhaler called a disk inhaler.

At school

Last winter Katy missed a lot of school because she kept having colds and her asthma got worse. When she came back, she had to catch up the work she'd missed. She found this quite hard, even though the teachers helped.

Now that Katy's asthma is under control she hardly ever has a day off but she still brings her reliever to school. She doesn't need it that often – mostly just before P.E. or swimming. Once, though, we got a fit of the giggles in class. Katy laughed so much she started coughing and wheezing. She had to use her reliever to help her breathe normally again.

If it's very cold or windy and Katy has a cold, she is allowed to stay indoors during break. The teachers know that this sort of weather, together with a cold, can make Katy's asthma symptoms worse. Other children with asthma or bad colds sometimes stay inside, too. If the weather's really chilly, I feel quite jealous of Katy, although she says she'd still rather be out in the playground with me.

On cold windy days, Katy wears a scarf across her face to warm the air going into her lungs. Cold air can trigger asthma symptoms.

Opposite: *Katy always carries her inhaler around with her, in a special shoulder bag bought by her mum.*

ASTHMA FACTS

WEATHER AND ASTHMA

Cold, dry air and strong winds can trigger asthma symptoms. Hot, humid days can also trigger asthma symptoms. This may be because levels of ozone (a kind of gas in the air) are often higher then.

Having an asthma attack

Last January, Katy had an asthma attack at school. Break had just finished and we were waiting in the classroom for the next lesson to start. Katy began to cough. She coughed and coughed, then wheezed and gasped for breath. She looked really scared. One of the boys ran to fetch our teacher, Miss Johnston. All the teachers in our school have been taught what to do if someone has an asthma attack. In the meantime, I took Katy's reliever inhaler out of her bag and gave it to her. She clicked on the inhaler and slowly sucked in the medicine.

I was very worried, but I kept talking to Katy to try and calm her down. Then Miss Johnston arrived with Katy's spare spacer. Luckily, Katy's medicine began to work. Soon, she stopped coughing and started to breathe normally. Miss Johnston told her to sit quietly until she felt completely better. After another ten minutes or so, Katy came back to her desk and joined in the rest of the lesson.

Opposite: **During Katy's asthma attack, Zara encouraged her to breathe slowly and deeply.**

Ten minutes after Katy took her reliever medicine she felt well enough to join in the lesson again.

ASTHMA FACTS

TREATING AN ASTHMA ATTACK

1 Find the person's inhaler and make sure they use it.
2 Call an adult, if there's one nearby.
3 Try to reassure the person that they will soon feel better.
   Don't put your arm around them – it may restrict their breathing even more.
4 Keep calm!
5 Tell them to breathe slowly and deeply.
6 Make sure they are sitting down. Don't let them lie down.
7 Loosen any tight clothing, and offer them a glass of water.

If, after five to ten minutes, they still cannot breathe properly and are feeling upset or very tired, call an ambulance. Make sure they use their inhaler every few minutes until the ambulance arrives.

Who gets asthma?

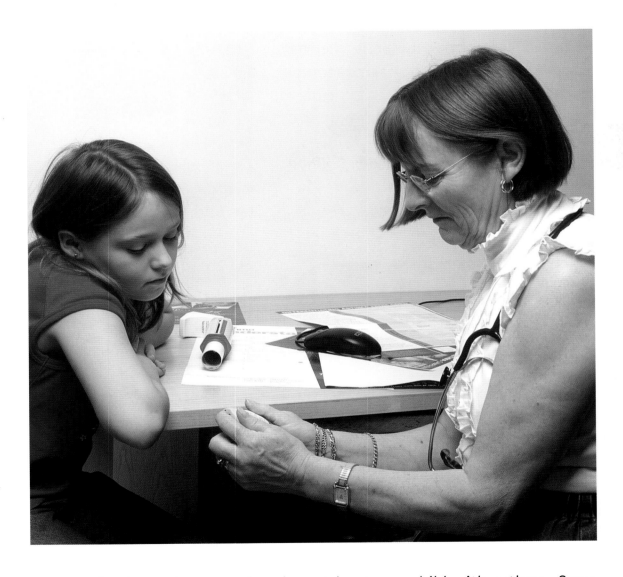

At our school, nearly every class has at least one child with asthma. Some children have mild symptoms and just cough or wheeze now and then. One or two have more severe symptoms, which sometimes make them quite ill.

Once, Matthew from Class 4 had to stay in hospital after a bad asthma attack and missed nearly a week of school.

Katy told me she's had asthma since she was four years old. At first everybody thought she just had lots of colds. Katy says she remembers how awful it was always to have a runny nose and a sore throat, even in summer. Her mum kept taking her to the doctor, but for a long time nobody was sure she had asthma. Katy says that's partly because there isn't a simple test to find out whether someone's got asthma or not.

Opposite: **Katy visits her doctor regularly to make sure that she is taking the right amount of medicine to control her asthma.**

ASTHMA FACTS

WHO GETS ASTHMA?

Around 150 million people in the world have asthma. Most people with asthma live in developed countries. Some people believe that our modern lifestyle, with its highly-processed foods, central heating and high levels of pollution, might be partly to blame.

A GROWING PROBLEM

Asthma is one of the main causes of ill health in children. Around one in eight children in the United Kingdom has asthma, although some children have more symptoms than others. More and more children are developing asthma and nobody knows for sure why this is.

Car exhaust fumes and other pollutants release gases into the air that can make asthma symptoms worse. When air pollution levels are high, anyone who has asthma is advised to stay indoors.

Hay fever and eczema

One time, when Katy and her mum went to the doctor, the doctor asked if any other members of the family had ever had asthma. She also asked if anyone suffered from **hay fever**. That's because people in the same family often have one or the other, or sometimes both.

Katy's mum has really bad hay fever, which is triggered by grass and pollen. During late spring and summer she's always sneezing. Her nose runs and her eyes are red and watery.

Eczema is related to asthma, too. Like asthma, eczema is often triggered by allergens such as house dust mites and pets with fur or feathers. Katy says Laura had eczema as a baby. Patches of skin inside her elbows and behind her knees became dry, scaly and itchy. Katy's mum had to wash Laura with special oily soaps and put cream on her skin. She also had to make sure Laura's room was as dust-free as possible.

Luckily, Laura grew out of her eczema by the time she was three years old. She's fine now – well as fine as little sisters go!

Opposite: **Katy's mum has hay fever. She takes medicine to relieve her symptoms when they are really bad.**

Pollen from grasses can trigger hay fever.

Katy's sister, Laura, used to have eczema when she was a baby.

ASTHMA FACTS

ECZEMA

Like asthma, eczema is also increasing. About one in eight children has eczema. Fortunately most children grow out of it by the time they are teenagers.

Having a sleepover

At night, Katy makes sure she has her reliever where she can reach it quickly.

Katy often comes to stay at weekends and during the holidays. My dad usually gets us a take-away pizza to eat while we watch a video. We like funny films best.

Before Katy arrives I help my mum vacuum the sitting room and my bedroom. We shake out the rugs and dust the furniture. If it's not too cold, we open the windows to let in some fresh air. We also give my dog, Molly, a bath and shut her into my mum's office. Poor Molly! She whines to be let out, but Katy's allergic to dogs and cats.

Katy always brings her medicines with her. Before bed, she takes her preventer, and makes sure she has her reliever nearby. So far, she's only had to use it once, when smoke from my dad's cigarette drifted upstairs. Since then, dad's given up smoking, which we're all glad about.

At first, we were all a bit nervous about Katy staying in case she had an asthma attack. But Katy never forgets to take her medicines, and her mum's told us what to do if there's an emergency. So now we don't worry at all.

Katy and I love sleepovers!

Molly could trigger Katy's asthma symptoms, so she is kept out of Katy's way.

ASTHMA FACTS

SMOKING AND ASTHMA

If a person with asthma smokes, their asthma symptoms will probably get much worse. Even if someone with asthma just breathes in smoke from another person's cigarette, they run a higher risk of having an asthma attack.

Going to the asthma clinic

Katy blows into a peak flow meter to test how open her airways are. If her peak flow score is lower than it should be, her treatment may need changing.

Every few months Katy goes to the clinic with her mum so that the asthma nurse can check that Katy's asthma is under control. Katy says:

"I quite like going to the asthma clinic. The nurses are kind and answer any questions I've got about my asthma. Last time I went, Janice was on duty. First, she weighed and measured me to make sure I'm growing properly. She said some children with asthma who are not on the right treatment cough so much during the night, their bodies don't get enough rest to develop as they should.

"She also measured how hard I could blow air out of my lungs. I took a huge breath and blew into a special tube called a **peak flow meter**. As I blew, a marker slid up the scale on the outside. Janice was pleased.

"'That's great!' she said. 'You can blow much harder now. Your asthma is really under control.'

"Janice also checked that I was using my inhaler correctly. I found this quite hard so Janice suggested I practise by playing some special breathing games at home. My favourite is when I have to suck sweets off a table with a straw, one at a time, and hold them up for at least 10 seconds. If I do it, mum lets me eat the sweets. I'm getting quite good now!"

Sucking up sweets with a straw is a fun way to practise sucking in air. Katy needs to be able to hold her breath for at least ten seconds if she is to use her inhalers correctly.

ASTHMA FACTS

KEEPING A DIARY

Children with asthma are encouraged to keep a diary of their asthma symptoms. Each day, they write down how much medicine they have had, and how they are feeling. If they have their own peak flow meters, they also record how hard they can blow out air. If their score regularly drops below a figure agreed at the last visit, they know it is time to visit the clinic again.

Best friends

Katy's my best friend. We laugh at the same things and like doing the same things. A few weeks ago, we both started learning the recorder. Katy's mum thought it would be good for Katy's asthma. Katy and I just think it's fun.

Katy never lets her asthma stop her doing what she wants. Even if she feels asthma symptoms coming on, she only stops for five minutes or so to take her reliever inhaler and wait for the medicine to work. Katy's very fit – fitter than me! When we go to the playground, she always says, "Race you!" and she nearly always wins. Katy says that when she's grown up, she wants to be a sports teacher.

I know that Katy is sometimes fed up with having asthma, but most of the time neither of us thinks about it at all. We're having too much fun!

Asthma need not stop anyone from enjoying all kinds of sport and exercise.

Opposite: **Some people believe that playing a wind instrument, such as a recorder, helps people with asthma control their breathing better.**

ASTHMA FACTS

ASTHMA AND SPORT

Many sportsmen and women have overcome asthma to excel in their field. They include the winner of the 2003 London Marathon, Paula Radcliffe; the footballer Paul Scholes, who plays for Manchester United and England; Austin Healey, who plays rugby for England; and the swimmer Karen Pickering, who won a gold medal at the 2002 Commonwealth Games.

Questions people ask

Q. **Do children with asthma grow out of it?**

A. It depends. About one in three children lose their asthma completely as they get older. Some people find their asthma improves when they become teenagers, but that it returns when they are adults.

Katy may grow out of her asthma when she is older.

Q. **Is there a cure for asthma?**

A. Not yet – although scientists have recently discovered a **gene** which is partly responsible for the development of asthma in children. It is hoped that further research will lead to new ways of diagnosing and treating asthma.

Q. **How many people in the United Kingdom have asthma?**

A. About 5.1 million people in the United Kingdom have asthma – that's one in eight children and one in thirteen adults. Worldwide, there are over 150 million people with asthma.

One in eight children in the United Kingdom has asthma.

Q. **Are there any sports that people with asthma shouldn't do?**

A. It's possible to do all kinds of sports. However, people with asthma should only take up scuba diving or high-altitude sports, such as skiing, mountaineering and hiking, if their asthma is completely under control.

Q. **Does where you live affect asthma symptoms?**

A. Although pollution is thought to be a common trigger, it is only one of many things that can affect asthma. So far, no one has proved that moving to a place with cleaner air helps asthma symptoms.

Q. **Can you have a pet if you have asthma?**

A. It depends on whether you are allergic to them. Over half of all children with asthma are allergic to dogs, cats and other animals with fur or feathers. Their symptoms are triggered by allergens in the animals' fur, saliva and urine that find their way into the air and are breathed in. Therefore, it's usually best not to keep a pet if you or someone in your house has asthma.

Swimming is a good form of exercise for children with asthma.

Q. **Do animals get asthma?**

A. Yes. Cats can get asthma, and their symptoms are similar to those of humans. Feline (cat) asthma is triggered by allergens in a cat's environment.

Glossary

airways Tiny branching tubes that carry air from the windpipe into the lungs. The tubes get smaller and smaller as they branch deeper into the lungs.

allergen A substance that causes an allergic reaction, making the body react badly.

allergy An abnormal reaction of the body to something that is usually harmless. For example, if someone has an allergy to dust or cats, they may get itchy eyes, a runny nose, or trouble with their breathing.

dose A measured amount of medicine. A doctor says how much medicine should be taken.

eczema A disease which makes parts of the skin red, itchy and scaly. Like asthma, eczema cannot be cured. However, it can be controlled with medicine and cream. You cannot catch eczema from anyone else.

gene A tiny unit found in every cell in our bodies which gives us special characteristics, such as hair colour. Genes are passed on from parents to their children.

hay fever Irritation in the nose, eyes and throat caused mainly by pollen from grasses. Symptoms include sneezing, a runny nose and sore, watering eyes.

house dust mite Microscopic creature (too small to be seen with the naked eye) that lives in the home in furniture and bedding, feeding mainly on dead skin cells. They are usually harmless, although their droppings and dead bodies may cause an allergic reaction in some people.

inhaler A device used to deliver asthma medicine so it can be breathed in, or inhaled. The asthma medicine can be a preventer or a reliever medicine.

mucus Slimy liquid that moistens and protects different parts of your body, such as the linings of your nose, mouth and airways.

peak flow meter A plastic tube with a marker on the outside used to measure how hard someone can blow out and therefore how well someone's lungs are working.

preventer A kind of asthma medicine used to soothe the airways in the lungs so that they are not so sensitive. It works quickly to prevent, or stop, the symptoms of asthma, making an asthma attack less likely to happen.

reliever A kind of asthma medicine used to relax the muscles around the airways in the lungs so that they open up, making it easier to breathe. It works quickly to relieve, or ease, the symptoms of asthma.

spacer Container that is fixed to an inhaler. Most children use a spacer with their inhaler. It is easier to use than just an inhaler by itself because you do not have to press the inhaler and breathe in at exactly the same time. It is also better at getting the asthma medicine into the lungs.

symptom Something felt by a person who has an illness or disease. For example, coughing and wheezing is a symptom of asthma.

trigger Something that sets off something else. For example, pollen or a cold may trigger, or cause, the symptoms of asthma.

windpipe Tube running from the back of the throat to the lungs. Air enters and leaves the body through the windpipe when we breathe in.

Useful organisations

**HERE ARE SOME ORGANISATIONS YOU MIGHT LIKE TO CONTACT
FOR MORE INFORMATION ABOUT ASTHMA**

NATIONAL ASTHMA CAMPAIGN
Providence House
Providence Place
London N1 0NT
Tel: 0207 226 2260

NATIONAL ASTHMA CAMPAIGN SCOTLAND
2a North Charlotte Street
Edinburgh EH2 4HR
Tel: 0131 226 2544

Asthma Campaign helpline telephone number:
0845 7 01 02 03

PEAK
(Holidays for children with asthma,
aged 6–17 years)
Tel: 020 7704 5892
Email: PEAK@asthma.org.uk

www.asthma.org.uk
*Gives plenty of news and information about asthma
and includes a section for children.*

ALLERGY UK
Deepdene House
30 Bellegrove Road
Welling, Kent DA16 3PY
Tel: 020 8303 8525
Helpline telephone number: 020 8303 8583
www.allergyfoundation.com
*Includes information about all kinds of allergies,
including asthma.*

BRITISH LUNG FOUNDATION
78 Hatton Garden
London EC1B 1PX
Tel: 020 7831 5831
www.lunguk.org
*Gives information about the charity's research into
lung disease and has a fact sheet on asthma.*

NATIONAL ECZEMA SOCIETY
Hill House
Highgate Hill
London N9 5NA
Tel: 020 7281 3553
Helpline telephone number: 0870 241 3604
www.eczema.org
*Gives information about eczema and includes links
to other sites*

OTHER WEBSITES

www.bbc.co.uk/health/asthma
*Gives general information about asthma, with
links to other sites.*

Index